My Science Library

Pull It, Push It

by Buffy Silverman

Science Content Editor:
Shirley Duke

Rourke
Educational Media

rourkeeducationalmedia.com

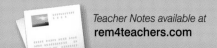

Teacher Notes available at rem4teachers.com

Science Content Editor: Shirley Duke holds a bachelor's degree in biology and a master's degree in education from Austin College in Sherman, Texas. She taught science in Texas at all levels for twenty-five years before starting to write for children. Her science books include *You Can't Wear These Genes, Infections, Infestations, and Diseases, Enterprise STEM, Forces and Motion at Work, Environmental Disasters,* and *Gases.* She continues writing science books and also works as a science content editor.

www.rourkeeducationalmedia.com

Photo credits: Cover © John93; Pages 2/3 © MANDY GODBEHEAR; Pages 4/5 © Thomas M Perkins; Pages 6/7 © Andreas Gradin; Pages 8/9 © MaszaS, Andrr; Pages 10/11 © Vaclav Volrab, Rena Schild; Pages 12/13 © Dimoza, SVLuma; Pages 14/15 © Francis Wong Chee Yen, Plus69, Laurent Renault; Pages 16/17 © Walter G Arce, crazy4design; Pages 18/19 © MANDY GODBEHEAR; Pages 20/21 © Mike Flippo, Alex Galea

Editor: Kelli Hicks

My Science Library series produced by Blue Door Publishing, Florida for Rourke Educational Media.

Library of Congress PCN Data

Silverman, Buffy
Pull It, Push It / Buffy Silverman
    p. cm. -- (My Science Library)
ISBN 978-1-61810-096-2 (Hard cover) (alk. paper)
ISBN 978-1-61810-229-4 (Soft cover)
Library of Congress Control Number: 2012930297

Rourke Educational Media
Printed in the United States of America,
North Mankato, Minnesota

Educational Media

rourkeeducationalmedia.com
customerservice@rourkeeducationalmedia.com • PO Box 643328 Vero Beach, Florida 32964

Table of Contents

Make It Move 4

Speed It Up 10

Slow Down and Stop 14

Forces Act Against One Another 18

Show What You Know 22

Glossary 23

Index 24

Make It Move

Every day you make objects move. In the morning you pick up a toothbrush, open and close a dresser drawer, grab a box of cereal, and lift your backpack. You pedal your bicycle and ride it to school. Your actions set your toothbrush, cereal box, and backpack in motion.

Milk flows when you lift and tilt a bottle.

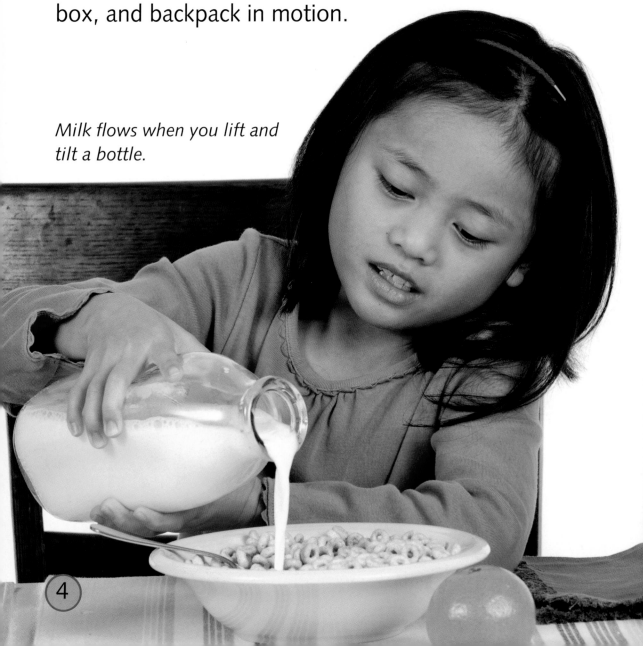

You use your muscles when you
make things move.

5

To move an object, you must exert a **force**. Tools and machines can also exert a force. They use a force to set something in motion. A force is a push or a pull. A push or a pull can cause an object to move. Once an object is moving, it needs a force to **speed** up, slow down, change direction, or stop.

The First Law of Motion

Sir Isaac Newton

Sir Isaac Newton was an English scientist who lived from 1642-1727. He discoved the laws of motion and the law of **gravity**. Newton's first law states that an object will not move unless a force acts on it. Once an object is moving, it keeps moving until another force acts to stop it.

A force is a push or a pull. You push a soccer ball with your foot to create the force that moves it down the field.

Without a push or pull, a basketball won't move. The tendency for objects to stay at rest or to keep moving is called **inertia**. Throw a ball and it soars to the basket. Your push overcomes the ball's inertia so the ball moves. Objects need a push or pull to stop moving, too. The ball's inertia would keep it moving. When you catch a ball, the force of your hands stops the ball from moving farther.

basketball and it flies through the air. Its forward
is stopped by the backboard, making the ball
directions. If the ball misses the backboard, the
f gravity pulls it back down.

Speed It Up

Have you ever raced on a bicycle? To make a bicycle go, you push on the pedals and spin them. To speed up, you push harder and faster. The greater the force you apply, the faster the bicycle moves. The speed that a bicycle travels is measured as the distance it travels in a certain amount of time.

When you push down on bicycle pedals, you move the chain. The chain turns the back wheel and makes the bicycle go.

Bicyclists use their muscles to create the force needed to move their bicycle faster when they race. The winner is the person who uses the greatest force over the distance.

11

Try to ride a bike with a basket filled with books. You must push hard to carry you and your heavy load. You move slowly with your load. As the **mass** of an object increases, you need more force to get it moving. That's why it takes a bigger push to roll a boulder than it does to roll a pebble!

You must push hard to move a massive ball.

It takes less force to move a ball with less mass.

The weight of the people riding behind the bicycle increases the load. The bicyclist must then increase his force by pedaling harder to overcome the load's inertia.

Slow Down and Stop

At the end of a bicycle race, a rider slows down. Force is needed to slow and stop a moving object. A bicyclist pulls brake levers which move brake pads. Brake pads squeeze against a wheel's rim, slowing the bike until it stops. The force of two surfaces rubbing against each other is called **friction**. Friction slows a moving object.

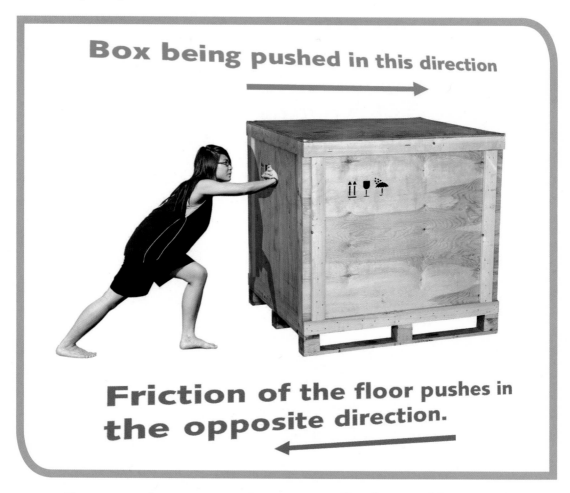

Box being pushed in this direction

Friction of the floor pushes in the opposite direction.

To move a box you must overcome the force of friction that acts in the opposite direction.

brake pad

Brake pads provide some of the friction needed to stop the bicycle. Without friction, a moving bike would never stop!

Even without braking, friction slows a bicycle or car. Tires rub against the road, slowing a vehicle. Air also rubs against moving objects. A racecar is designed so that there is less friction to slow it down. It has few sharp edges which means it has less wind resistance. Air slips over its smooth, streamlined surface.

Air trapped in parachutes slows a drag racing car by increasing friction with the air to form an opposing force.

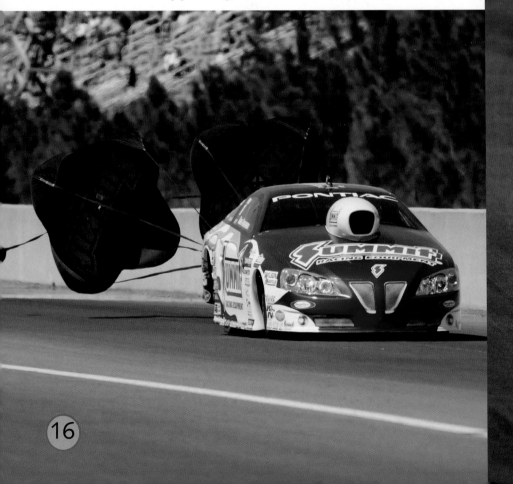

A racecar speeds around a track. Its smooth, sleek shape lets air flow over and under it to reduce friction so it will go faster.

Forces Act Against One Another

Watch a game of tug-of-war. One boy pulls a rope, trying to move the other boy. The other boy pulls in the opposite direction. These forces act against each other.

direction of force

Both boys feel the rope pulling against them. If both boys pull with the same force, neither one moves. Then the forces are in **balance**.

direction of force

The boy with more force wins a game of tug-of-war.

Forces act in pairs. One force may move an object forward, while another force acts in the opposite direction. A skateboarder pushes her foot behind her board. The board rolls forward, moving in the opposite direction of her push. The forward movement is a **reaction** to the rider's backward push.

backward push   **forward motion**

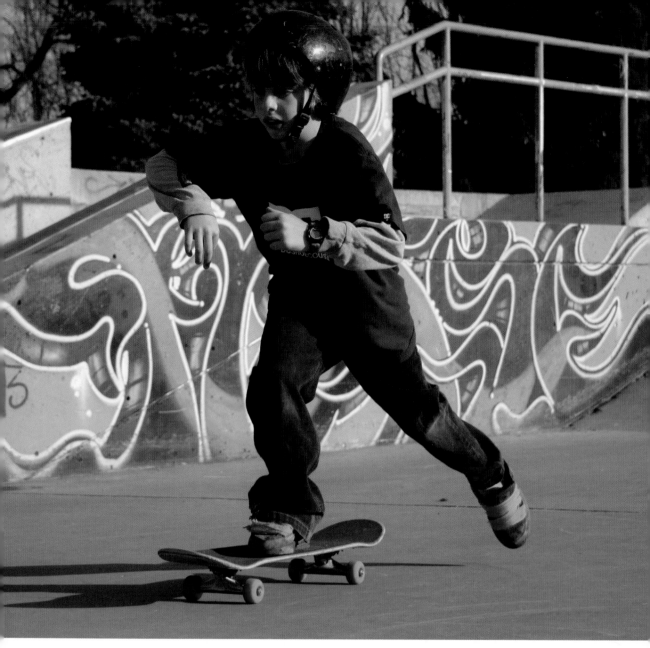

If the rider wants to go faster, he'll have to push with more force. The forward motion will be as fast as the force of the backward motion.

Every day you push and pull objects. You use tools to make things move and make them stop. Think of all the ways you create forces!

Show What You Know

1. What is needed to make an object move?

2. Why can't you throw a bowling ball as far as a baseball?

3. When you pull the paddle back, what direction does a kayak move?

Glossary

balance (BAL-uhnss): equal amount of force on both sides

force (FORSS): any action that pulls or pushes something else

friction (FRIK-shuhn): a force that slows down objects when they rub against each other

gravity (GRAV-uh-tee): the force that pulls things down toward the Earth

inertia (in-UR-shuh): resistance of an object to any change in motion. Inertia makes it hard to get something moving that is still, and makes it hard to stop an object that is moving.

mass (MASS): the amount of matter that an object contains

reaction (re-AK-shuhn): an action or response to something that has happened

speed (SPEED): the rate at which something moves

Index

force   6, 7, 8, 9, 10, 11, 12, 13,
   14, 16, 18, 19, 20, 21
friction   14, 15, 16, 17
gravity   6, 9
mass   12
motion   4, 6, 9, 20
Newton, Isaac   6

reaction   20
pull(s)   6, 7, 8, 9, 14,
   18, 19, 21
push   6, 7, 8, 9, 10, 12,
   20, 21
speed   6, 10

Websites to Visit

www.exploratorium.edu/skateboarding/trick.html
www.sciencebob.com/experiments/the_lincoln_dive.php
www.sciencetoymaker.org/balloon/index.html

About the Author

Buffy Silverman writes science and nature books for children. She learns more about the world with each new subject she writes about.

Ask The Author!
www.rem4students.com

24